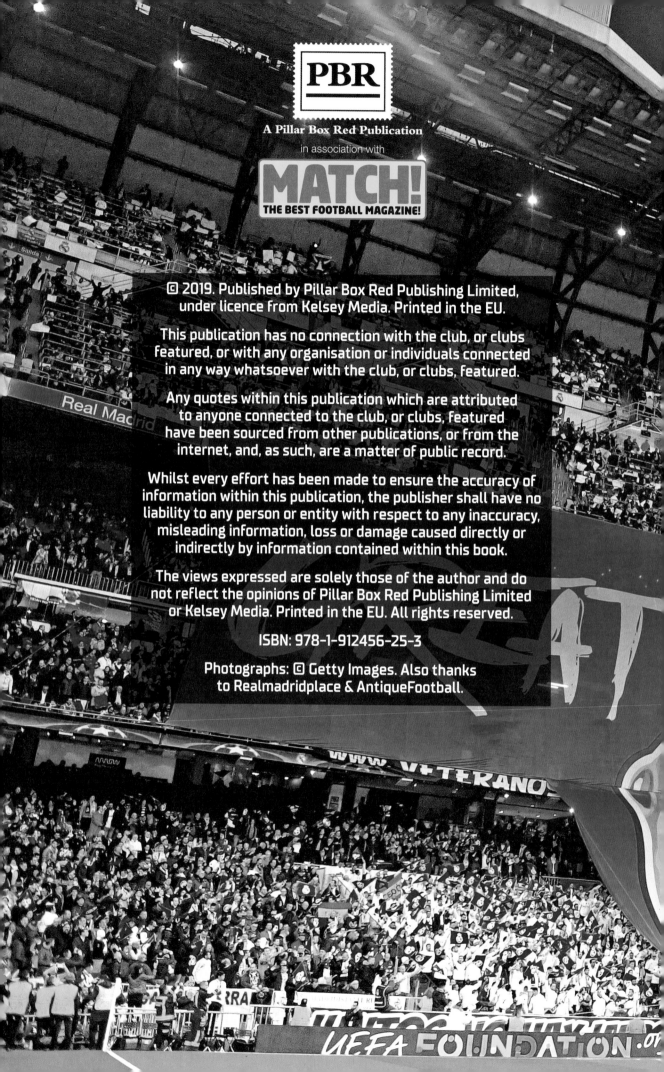

PBR

A Pillar Box Red Publication

in association with

MATCH!
THE BEST FOOTBALL MAGAZINE!

ISBN: 978-1-912456-25-3

Photographs: © Getty Images. Also thanks to Realmadridplace & AntiqueFootball.

MATCH!
THE BEST FOOTBALL MAGAZINE!

REAL MADRID ANNUAL 2020

Written by
Tim O'Sullivan

Edited by
Stephen Fishlock

Designed by
Darryl Tooth

CONTENTS

SEASON REVIEW

We look back at Real Madrid's 2018-19 campaign month by month, checking out their big moments, star players and more!

AUGUST

MEGA MOMENTS!

Ramos celebrates in front of the Atletico supporters

Just months after picking up a mind-blowing 13th Champions League trophy, Real Madrid played in the UEFA Super Cup against Europa League winners Atletico Madrid. Sadly for Los Blancos, goals by Sergio Ramos and Karim Benzema couldn't stop their local rivals winning 4-2 after extra-time!

Carvajal opens Real's account for the season

Real started their 2018-19 La Liga campaign with a comfortable 2-0 win against Getafe. You would have expected Gareth Bale or Karim Benzema to be Los Blancos' first goalscorer of the new season, but it was wicked right-back Dani Carvajal. What a star!

Benzema slots home against Girona

Los Blancos finished August with their second La Liga win after smashing Girona 4-1. Sergio Ramos opened the scoring with a penalty and Wales legend Gareth Bale also got on the scoresheet, but Karim Benzema was the star of the show with a double!

MAN OF THE MONTH!

GARETH BALE The Welsh wing wizard was on fire during pre-season, and he started the proper season in the same form! His goals in Real Madrid's first two La Liga games v Getafe and Girona were class!

DID YOU KNOW?

Bale scored in three pre-season games in a row between August 4 and August 11. Italian giants Juventus, Roma and AC Milan were his victims!

REAL'S RESULTS

15/08	USC	Real Madrid	2-4	Atletico Madrid
19/08	LIGA	Real Madrid	2-0	Getafe
26/08	LIGA	Girona	1-4	Real Madrid

SEPTEMBER

MEGA MOMENTS!

Benzema and Ramos get on the scoresheet again

Something bonkers happened at the Bernabeu at the start of September! Just six days after blitzing Girona 4-1 in La Liga, Real Madrid smashed Leganes by exactly the same scoreline. And, wait for it... the exact same goalscorers. Now how crazy is that?

Los Blancos began their quest for a record 14th Champions League crown with a comfortable 3-0 win against Serie A giants Roma. Isco and Bale found the net, but the moment of the match arrived when Mariano Diaz curled an epic 30-yard stunner into the top corner!

Thumbs up for Mariano

Asensio's on target

Real were locked in a scrappy La Liga game against Espanyol, but managed to nick all three points after an absolutely devastating left-footed finish by Marco Asensio. The Spain wonderkid didn't celebrate the inch-perfect drive, as he once played on loan at Espanyol!

REAL'S RESULTS

01/09	LIGA	Real Madrid	4-1	Leganes
15/09	LIGA	Athletic Bilbao	1-1	Real Madrid
19/09	UCL	Real Madrid	3-0	Roma
22/09	LIGA	Real Madrid	1-0	Espanyol
26/09	LIGA	Sevilla	3-0	Real Madrid
29/09	LIGA	Real Madrid	0-0	Atletico Madrid

MAN OF THE MONTH!

SERGIO RAMOS Real Madrid's iconic captain started September with a goal against Leganes, then ended the month with a world-class display against arch rivals Atletico Madrid. His rock-solid defending helped keep the derby locked at 0-0!

DID YOU KNOW?

Real's 3-0 thrashing by Sevilla was their first La Liga defeat since losing to the same team in 2017-18!

OCTOBER

MEGA MOMENTS!

Marcelo bags against Viktoria Plzen

Real needed to get back on track in the Champions League after a shock 1-0 defeat to CSKA Moscow – and they did just that with a 2-1 win against Viktoria Plzen on CL matchday three. Legendary Real and Brazil left-back Marcelo scored the second goal!

Julen Lopetegui was sacked as Real Madrid manager after Los Blancos suffered a humiliating 5-1 defeat to massive rivals Barcelona in El Clasico. It capped off a terrible 2018 for Lopetegui, who was also sacked by Spain just days before the World Cup!

Lopetegui gets the boot

Odriozola impresses

October was a shocking month for Los Blancos, but they ended it well with a 4-0 win against Melilla in the Copa del Rey. Exciting wonderkids Alvaro Odriozola and Cristo Gonzalez hit the headlines by finding the net in a comfortable victory!

REAL'S RESULTS

02/10	UCL	CSKA Moscow	1-0	Real Madrid
06/10	LIGA	Alaves	1-0	Real Madrid
20/10	LIGA	Real Madrid	1-2	Levante
23/10	UCL	Real Madrid	2-1	Viktoria Plzen
28/10	LIGA	Barcelona	5-1	Real Madrid
31/10	CDR	Melilla	0-4	Real Madrid

MAN OF THE MONTH!

MARCELO The Brazil superstar's main job is to defend, but he chipped in with top-quality goals against Levante, Barcelona and Viktoria Plzen! Most strikers would be happy scoring three games in a row, so for a left-back to do it is extra special!

DID YOU KNOW?

The 5-1 humiliation against Barcelona was Real's biggest defeat in El Clasico since losing 5-0 in 2010!

NOVEMBER

MEGA MOMENTS!

Solari gets the top job

Real Madrid appointed Santiago Solari as manager on a three-year deal in November. Los Blancos were looking for a new boss after sacking Julen Lopetegui in October but, instead of looking outside, decided to promote Solari from Real's B team, Castilla!

REAL'S RESULTS

03/11	LIGA	Real Madrid	2-0	Real Valladolid
07/11	UCL	Viktoria Plzen	0-5	Real Madrid
11/11	LIGA	Celta Vigo	2-4	Real Madrid
24/11	LIGA	Eibar	3-0	Real Madrid
27/11	UCL	Roma	0-2	Real Madrid

Bale gets congratulated by his team-mates

Los Blancos secured their spot in the Champions League knockout stages with two wicked Group G wins in November. They demolished Czech Republic champions Viktoria Plzen 5-0 away from home, then beat Roma 2-0 at the Stadio Olimpico!

MAN OF THE MONTH!

KARIM BENZEMA Real's long-serving goal king continued his red-hot form with a November to remember! The French striker bagged twice against Viktoria Plzen in the Champo League, then scored another in the 4-2 win against Celta Vigo. Hero!

DID YOU KNOW?

The 5-0 destruction of Viktoria Plzen was Real's biggest away win in the Champions League since smashing Cyprus' APOEL 6-0 in November 2017!

DECEMBER

MEGA MOMENTS!

Bale's on fire

Gareth Bale showed his class with an outrageous finish against Huesca. A cross was floated into the box from the right wing, and the Wales superstar sprinted on to the ball and crashed an unstoppable volley into the bottom corner. Worldy!

REAL'S RESULTS

01/12	LIGA	Real Madrid	2-0	Valencia
06/12	CDR	Real Madrid	6-1	Melilla
09/12	LIGA	Huesca	0-1	Real Madrid
12/12	UCL	Real Madrid	0-3	CSKA Moscow
15/12	LIGA	Real Madrid	1-0	Rayo Vallecano
19/12	CWC	Kashima Antlers	1-3	Real Madrid
22/12	CWC	Real Madrid	4-1	Al Ain

Real lift the FIFA Club World Cup yet again

Real Madrid won the FIFA Club World Cup for the third year in a row in December! Gareth Bale scored a quality hat-trick in the semi-final against Kashima Antlers, then Los Blancos sealed the trophy with a crushing 4-1 win against UAE's Al Ain in the final!

MAN OF THE MONTH!

GARETH BALE The wicked winger must love Christmas, because he was pumped up the whole month! The Welsh icon bagged a ruthless hat-trick in the FIFA Club World Cup semi-final and netted the winner against Huesca in La Liga. Unstoppable!

DID YOU KNOW?

Real Madrid have now won the FIFA Club World Cup more than any other team in history! They were tied on three victories with Clasico rivals Barcelona, but December's triumph made it four!

JANUARY

MEGA MOMENTS!

Real Madrid were drawing away at Real Betis in La Liga with just two minutes to go – step forward Dani Ceballos. The highly-rated Spain wonderkid had the confidence to step up and take a crucial free-kick in the 88th minute, then slammed it home to give Los Blancos a 2-1 win!

Ceballos gets the plaudits

Real Madrid picked up another massive three points at home to top-four rivals Sevilla in January. Real dominated the game, but couldn't find the breakthrough, until defensive midfielder Casemiro smashed a 35-yard thunderbolt off the bar and in! The game finished 2-0!

Casemiro's the hero

Striker Karim Benzema's dynamite double helped Real Madrid win a six-goal thriller away to Espanyol at the end of the month! Sergio Ramos and Gareth Bale also scored, before Raphael Varane saw red in a true La Liga classic!

Benzema bags a brace

REAL'S RESULTS

03/01	LIGA	Villarreal	2-2	Real Madrid
06/01	LIGA	Real Madrid	0-2	Real Sociedad
09/01	CDR	Real Madrid	3-0	Leganes
13/01	LIGA	Real Betis	1-2	Real Madrid
16/01	CDR	Leganes	1-0	Real Madrid
19/01	LIGA	Real Madrid	2-0	Sevilla
24/01	CDR	Real Madrid	4-2	Girona
27/01	LIGA	Espanyol	2-4	Real Madrid
31/01	CDR	Girona	1-3	Real Madrid

MAN OF THE MONTH!

LUKA MODRIC A few weeks after picking up the iconic Ballon d'Or, Croatia magic man Modric showed the world why he became the first player to beat Cristiano Ronaldo and Lionel Messi to the prize since 2007. He dominated games for Real in January and scored a class goal against Sevilla!

DID YOU KNOW?

Karim Benzema scored five goals for Real Madrid between January 24 and January 31. He was on fire!

FEBRUARY

MEGA MOMENTS!

Vazquez nets v Barcelona

Lucas Vazquez had the greatest moment of his Real career so far with the opening goal in Madrid's Copa del Rey clash against Barcelona. Vazquez silenced the Nou Camp with some clever movement and a cool finish!

Real Madrid were in decent form heading into their crunch La Liga clash with Atletico Madrid, and they beat their rivals with an epic 3-1 away win. Casemiro and Sergio Ramos put Los Blancos 2-1 up, before Gareth Bale's left-foot rocket sealed the victory – his 100th goal for the club!

100-up for Bale

Asensio sinks Ajax

Real's Champions League last 16 clash with Ajax ended in tears in the second leg, but they were awesome in the first 90 minutes. The 13-time champions won the first leg 2-1 in Amsterdam, thanks to quality goals from Karim Benzema and Marco Asensio!

MAN OF THE MONTH!

CASEMIRO The Brazil anchorman was a rock for Real in February. He bossed midfields all month, and even chipped in with a goal against Atletico!

DID YOU KNOW?

The latest Madrid derby was Real's 12th away win at Atletico in their last 18 La Liga clashes. They'd drawn five and only lost one of the other six!

REAL'S RESULTS

03/02	LIGA	Real Madrid	3-0	Alaves
06/02	CDR	Barcelona	1-1	Real Madrid
09/02	LIGA	Atletico Madrid	1-3	Real Madrid
13/02	UCL	Ajax	1-2	Real Madrid
17/02	LIGA	Real Madrid	1-2	Girona
24/02	LIGA	Levante	1-2	Real Madrid
27/02	CDR	Real Madrid	0-3	Barcelona

MARCH
MEGA MOMENTS!

Varane pokes home his second goal of the season

Real got over a week of heartbreaking defeats to Barcelona and Ajax with a massive bounceback win against Real Valladolid in La Liga. Los Blancos won 4-1 away from home thanks to goals by Raphael Varane, Modric and a quality Benzema double!

REAL'S RESULTS

02/03	LIGA	Real Madrid	0-1	Barcelona
05/03	UCL	Real Madrid	1-4	Ajax
10/03	LIGA	Real Valladolid	1-4	Real Madrid
16/03	LIGA	Real Madrid	2-0	Celta Vigo
31/03	LIGA	Real Madrid	3-2	Huesca

Los Blancos picked up where they left off against Real Valladolid with a mega confident 2-0 win against Celta Vigo. Isco opened the scoring with a close-range finish, before a rare right-footed goal from Bale sealed the win late on!

Bale scores again

Zidane returns

Real Madrid legend Zinedine Zidane returned as manager on March 11 after Santiago Solari was sacked. The iconic Frenchman won the Champions League once with Real as a player and three times with the club as a gaffer. They simply had to bring Zizou back!

MAN OF THE MONTH!

ISCO The creative genius was playing footy from a different planet in March! He destroyed opponents with his clever dribbling and turns, and scored vital league goals against Huesca and Celta Vigo. Hero!

DID YOU KNOW?

The crushing 4-1 defeat to Ajax meant it was the first time Real failed to reach the Champions League quarter-finals since the 2009-10 season!

APRIL
MEGA MOMENTS!

Benzema turns it around against Eibar

After losing 2-1 to Valencia – Zinedine Zidane's first defeat since returning as Madrid manager – Real were in trouble again at 1-0 down to Eibar. But Karim Benzema inspired an epic second-half comeback with another double to thrill the Bernabeu fans!

Striker Karim Benzema was arguably Real Madrid's best player in 2018-19, and his finest moment arrived in April against Athletic Bilbao. The Frenchman slammed home a totally unstoppable hat-trick as Real battered their La Liga rivals 3-0!

Hat-trick hero Benzema

MAN OF THE MONTH!

KARIM BENZEMA There's only one candidate for April! Benzema scored seven goals in his first four games of the month, including a hat-trick v Bilbao! That took his La Liga tally for the season to 21 – his second-best performance in ten years at the club!

DID YOU KNOW?

The win against Athletic Bilbao was Real Madrid's 90th El Viejo derby La Liga victory!

REAL'S RESULTS

03/04	LIGA	Valencia	2-1	Real Madrid
06/04	LIGA	Real Madrid	2-1	Eibar
15/04	LIGA	Leganes	1-1	Real Madrid
21/04	LIGA	Real Madrid	3-0	Athletic Bilbao
25/04	LIGA	Getafe	0-0	Real Madrid
28/04	LIGA	Rayo Vallencano	1-0	Real Madrid

Mariano at the double for Real against Villarreal

MAY

MEGA MOMENTS!

Madrid's final victory of the season came against Villarreal at the Bernabeu. Dominican Republic hero Mariano Diaz scored a class double and defender Jesus Vallejo bagged the other as Real won 3-2!

Vallejo celebrates his first ever Real Madrid goal

Zidane shouts instructions from the touchline

Los Blancos finished the season with defeats to Sociedad and Betis, but their campaign was over and Zidane had tested loads of younger players. They ended 2018-19 in third place with 68 points, 19 points behind Spanish champions Barcelona.

MAN OF THE MONTH!

MARIANO DIAZ The Dominican Republic striker didn't rock the Bernabeu like he intended to after arriving from Lyon in August 2018, but he still had some decent moments in 2018-19. Zidane gave him the chance to shine in May, and he rewarded the gaffer with a classy double against Villarreal!

DID YOU KNOW?

Real Madrid's final tally of 68 points was their poorest performance in a La Liga season since 2001-02!

REAL'S RESULTS

Date	Comp	Home	Score	Away
05/05	LIGA	Real Madrid	3-2	Villarreal
12/05	LIGA	Real Sociedad	3-1	Real Madrid
19/05	LIGA	Real Madrid	0-2	Real Betis

HAZARD
NEW GALACTICO

Belgium's demon dribbler is ready to become a Real Madrid icon!

Every football fan on the planet was getting bored of the Eden Hazard to Real Madrid transfer rumours, because nothing ever happened. But in June 2019, all that changed! Real Madrid completed the one signing they were desperate to make for years and Hazard finally got the chance to play for his dream club. But the move isn't just a dream for the Belgium megastar – Los Blancos supporters are in dreamland too, because now they feel like they've finally got the replacement for Cristiano Ronaldo that they failed to sign in the summer of 2018. If Hazard can live up to his monster £89 million price-tag, and the mega reputation he got for his world-class displays week-in week-out for Chelsea, he could be just as much as a talisman for Real as CR7 was during his goal-packed career at the Bernabeu!

DYNAMITE DRIBBLER

Real fans are in for a treat this season, because Hazard is probably the best dribbler in world football right now! Supporters might feel like they know him from watching Prem games on TV, but seeing Eden up close and live in the stadium is a whole new ball game. It's almost unfair how easy it is for Hazard to turn defenders inside out – and Madrid fans will get to see that every week now!

BELGIUM SUPERSTAR

Eden was unlucky not to win the Golden Ball at the 2018 World Cup. Eventual winner and new club team-mate Luka Modric was a deserved Player of the Tournament for his wicked displays for Croatia, but Hazard ran him close. The Belgian ripped up the tournament, scoring three goals, and will be hoping a great season in Spain can propel him to similar performances at Euro 2020!

PREMIER LEAGUE LEGEND

Chelsea splashed out £32 million to sign Hazard from French club Lille in 2012 and it looked a lot of money at the time. Fast-forward seven years and it looks like one of the biggest bargains in transfer history – especially after they sold him for nearly three times that amount! Hazard became a true Premier League icon, winning two titles, scoring 85 goals and bagging 54 assists!

PLAYING FOR HIS HERO

Joining Real Madrid is one of the greatest achievements for any professional footballer, but it's extra special for Hazard... and that's because his new gaffer was also his boyhood hero. Hazard grew up watching Zinedine Zidane, and studied how he destroyed opponents – and now he gets to impress his idol with his own legendary skills every single week. Now that's a dream come true!

FACTPACK

Position: Winger

Country: Belgium

D.O.B: 07/01/1991

Height: 5ft 9in

Boots: Nike Mercurial Vapor

Instagram: hazardeden_10

REAL MADRID BRAIN-BUSTER!

Can you answer these teasers correctly?

1. How many times have Real Madrid won the Champions League?

2. Who was Real's captain before Sergio Ramos took the armband in 2015?

3. Who scored two goals for Real in the 2018 Champions League final against Liverpool?

4. Ex-goalkeeper Keylor Navas plays international footy for which country?

5. What shirt number does Croatia magic man Luka Modric wear for the club?

6. Which homegrown hero scored Real's fourth goal in the 2017 Champions League final?

7. El Clasico is the name of their massive games against which fierce La Liga rival?

8. Real Madrid signed Gareth Bale and Luka Modric from which Premier League club?

9. Which Brazil hero wears the No.14 shirt at the Bernabeu?

10. Real Madrid won their 12th Champions League title in which British city?

1 ....
2 ....
3 ....
4 ....
5 ....
6 ....
7 ....
8 ....
9 ....
10 ....

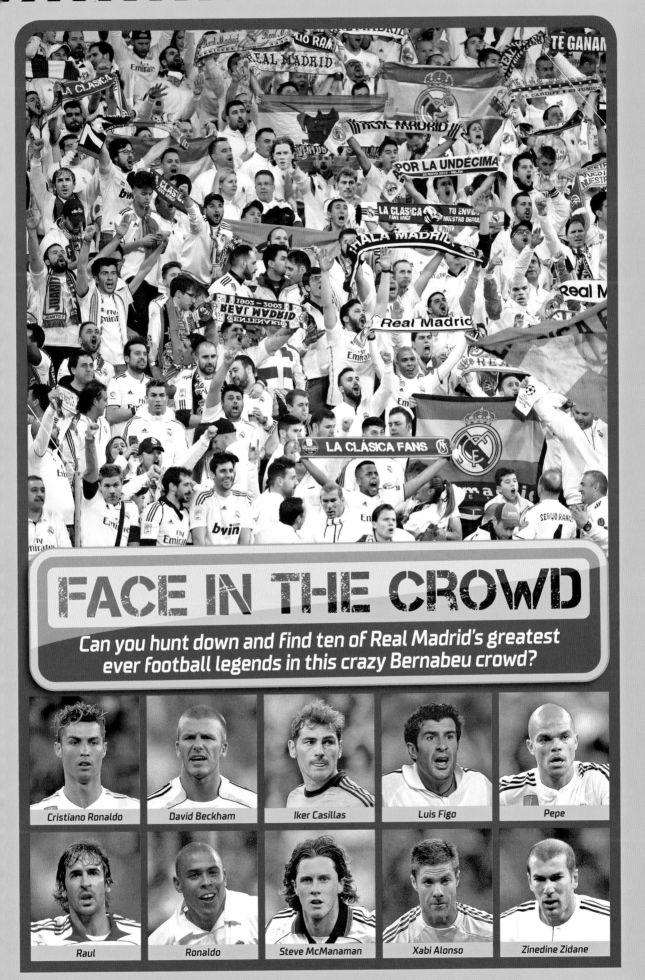

FACE IN THE CROWD

Can you hunt down and find ten of Real Madrid's greatest ever football legends in this crazy Bernabeu crowd?

Cristiano Ronaldo

David Beckham

Iker Casillas

Luis Figo

Pepe

Raul

Ronaldo

Steve McManaman

Xabi Alonso

Zinedine Zidane

ANSWERS ON PAGE 60

BERNABEU IN PICS!

Check out these awesome snaps of Real Madrid's iconic stadium!

The legendary ground holds over 80,000 fans, and it's hosted World Cup, Champions League and European Championship finals!

The Bernabeu has an awesome 'best club ever room', which features trophies and iconic moments from the club's history!

FACTFILE

Built: 1947

Capacity: 81,044

Nearest Neighbour: Atletico Madrid

First Match: Real Madrid 3-1 Belenenses, 1947

Record Attendance: 129,690 v AC Milan, 1956

The home changing room has separate sections for each player, including their own full-length picture and shirt number!

The benches for Real Madrid's coaches and substitutes are out of this world – they're like futuristic Formula 1 driver seats!

Real Madrid are adding a roof to the stadium, plus loads of restaurants and shops around it, which should be ready by the 2023-24 season!

The Bernabeu pitch is in perfect condition, and the person in charge of it used to be Arsenal's head groundsman!

The club museum is incredible! It's packed with loads of famous trophies and is the third most visited museum in Madrid!

MENDY

FLYING FULL-BACK

The left-back is ready to take over from Marcelo at the Bernabeu!

When Real Madrid started to rebuild last summer with a whole new set of Galacticos following one of their poorest seasons in recent memory, a new left-back wasn't on every Los Blancos fan's agenda. But with club legend Marcelo not getting any younger and a French influence already instilled through the spine of the club in manager Zinedine Zidane and club legends Karim Benzema and Raphael Varane, the £47 million signing of Ferland Mendy wasn't that much of a surprise. Brazilian legend Marcelo has been one of the greatest left-backs in the history of footy, but after an awesome run of form with Lyon, there's a new kid in town – and he's ready to take the Samba Star's crown. He might not be the biggest signing of Real's summer, but lightning-quick left-back Mendy could end up becoming one of their best!

LIGHTNING PACE

Mendy's like a winger the way he bursts up and down the left flank! He grew up in Le Havre's academy, who always produce rapid stars full of athleticism – and Mendy's no different. With loads of top French left-backs around at the minute in Lucas Hernandez, Benjamin Mendy and Lucas Digne, Ferland is hoping his move to Madrid will take him to the top of the national team pecking order!

DREAM TEAM

Mendy was included in the Ligue 1 Team of the Year in 2017-18, but despite calls for him to be named in France's 2018 World Cup squad, he failed to make the cut. After featuring in the Team of the Year again in 2018-19 ahead of left-backs from PSG, Lille and Marseille, he made himself a permanent fixture in the national team squad – and earned a massive-money move to Real Madrid!

INCREDIBLE RECOVERY

Mendy was told by doctors he might never play football ever again after having serious hip surgery when he was just 15. He was in a wheelchair for over six months and went back to hospital loads of times to make sure he could walk again. That determination has served him well during his football career so far, and fighting spirit like that will make him a big fans' favourite at Real!

TOP TACKLER

The France superstar is a modern left-back full of athleticism, pace and power, but he's still got classic old-fashioned tackling skills which rock wingers out of their boots! He doesn't give wide attacking players an inch of space and is rock-hard in one-on-ones, which is the one attribute that could see him edge Marcelo out of Real's first-choice XI during the 2019-20 season!

FACTPACK

Position: Left-back
Country: France
D.O.B: 08/06/1995
Height: 5ft 11in
Boots: Nike PhantomVSN
Instagram: ferland_mendy

AMAZING You Tube CLIPS!

Get a load of some of the coolest videos on REAL MADRID's official YouTube channel! You have to watch these...

REAL MADRID QR CODES EXPLAINED

This is a QR code – just scan it with your phone or tablet to watch each video clip on YouTube. Here's how to do it:

 Download and install a free QR Code reader from the app or android store.

 Hold your phone or tablet over the QR code and you'll be sent to the clip. Easy!

▶ ⏭ 1:35 / 8:12   HD 🔊 ⛶

▶ Thank You, Ron!

Cristiano Ronaldo had an unbelievable career with Real Madrid, packed with wondergoals and trophies, and Los Blancos thanked him for his service with this incredible six-minute video after he joined Juventus. Some of the skills, goals and big moments have to be seen to be believed. Proper Real legend!

▶ Future Of The Bernabeu!

This jaw-dropping video shows what the Bernabeu stadium will look like in the future. There's an epic silver roof, which looks like a spaceship, plus loads of awesome new rooms inside the stadium. Check it out!

▶ ⏭ 1:35 / 8:12   HD 🔊 ⛶

HD 🔊 ⛶ 1:35 / 8:12

▶ Up In The Air!

Real Madrid made the most of their sponsorship with Fly Emirates last December, because they were flown out first class to the 2018 FIFA Club World Cup in Abu Dhabi. Los Blancos' YouTube team got mind-blowing access to the players and Fly Emirates stuff during the flight!

HD 🔊 ⛶ 1:35 / 8:12

▶ Nou Camp Memories!

El Clasico is the most famous game in world footy, so Real have made a video of their best goals against Barcelona at the Nou Camp. Raul's dink and 'Ssshhh...' celebration is one of our favourites, but don't miss stunners from Steve McManaman, Ronaldo, Zinedine Zidane and Julio Baptista!

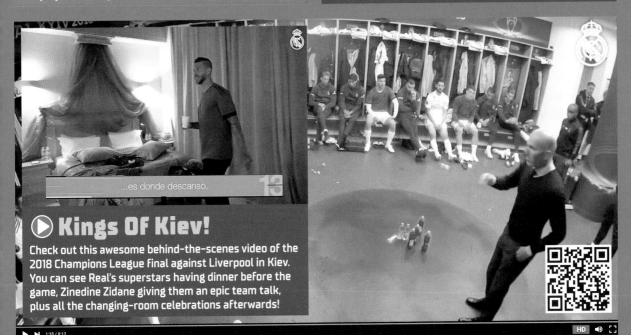

...es donde descanso. 13

▶ Kings Of Kiev!

Check out this awesome behind-the-scenes video of the 2018 Champions League final against Liverpool in Kiev. You can see Real's superstars having dinner before the game, Zinedine Zidane giving them an epic team talk, plus all the changing-room celebrations afterwards!

HD 🔊 ⛶ 1:35 / 8:12

HD 🔊 ⛶ 1:35 / 8:12

▶ Brilliant Bale!

Gareth Bale scored an absolutely mind-boggling goal against Barcelona in the 2014 Copa del Rey Final, and it's got nearly 12 million views on Real Madrid's official YouTube channel! Bale showed the fitness of Sir Mo Farah and the pace of Usain Bolt, then finished brilliantly. Epic strike!

HD 🔊 ⛶ 1:35 / 8:12

▶ Welcome Hazard!

No club in world footy does new-signing presentations like Real Madrid! Los Blancos finally signed Eden Hazard from Chelsea for £89 million in June after years of gossip and speculation, and they celebrated with a huge party at the Bernabeu. This live stream captured all of the magic!

SERGIO RAMOS

REAL MADRID LEGEND!

Sergio Ramos became only the seventh player to make 600 Real Madrid appearances last season! Here are five reasons why he's such an icon...

1

TOP TACKLER!

Footy's most entertaining players are usually strikers or midfielders, but Ramos puts defenders on the map with his exciting defensive style. His passion, aggression and no-nonsense tackling rock the boots off attackers! His battles with Antoine Griezmann and Mohamed Salah in recent Champions League Finals were unmissable!

2

LEGENDARY LEADER!

There was only one man who could take the captain's armband at Real after Iker Casillas left the club in 2015. Ramos oozed passion, charisma, desire and quality from day one at the Bernabeu, and he was always going to be the perfect replacement for Casillas. He went on to win three Champions League trophies in a row as captain!

RAMOS SEASON BY SEASON

	2005-06	2006-07
La Liga games	33	33
La Liga goals	4	5
Trophies won	0	1

3

SURPRISE GOAL KING!

Ramos isn't just a top defender – he gets involved in the other 18-yard box too. He scored seven La Liga goals in 2016-17 and six in 2018-19, but his most famous strike arrived in the 2014 Champions League final when he bagged a dramatic 93rd-minute equaliser against rivals Atletico Madrid! Real went on to win 4-1 in extra-time!

4

EPIC FOOTY BRAIN!

Ramos grabs the headlines for his amazing battles with strikers and last-minute goals, but people can't forget how clever he is at the back. The way he reads the game is incredible. If strikers are thinking about a flick, shot or bit of movement, you just know Ramos is predicting it well in advance. The Spaniard's such a classy defender!

5

BIG-GAME PLAYER!

How many times do you see awesome players destroy smaller teams in the league, then fail to show up in the big games? You get none of that from Ramos – he's the king of big matches! He shows his class on the biggest stages, including four Champions League finals, two European Championship finals and a World Cup final!

2007-08
La Liga games	33
La Liga goals	5
Trophies won	2

2008-09
La Liga games	32
La Liga goals	4
Trophies won	1

TURN OVER FOR MORE STATS!

CHAMPIONS LEAGUE KING!

Ramos absolutely bosses the Champo League every season! Here are some of his most memorable moments in the competition...

CHAMPO LEAGUE DEBUT!

September 13, 2005

Ramos made his Champions League debut in the 2005-06 season v French champs Lyon. He scored his first goal in the tournament against Olympiacos later that campaign, before Real Madrid crashed out to Arsenal in the last 16!

CHAMPIONS LEAGUE FACTPACK

Games: 119 ★ Goals: 11

Yellow Cards: 38 ★ Red Cards: 3

Winners' Medals: 4

FIRST CL TROPHY!

May 24, 2014

His wait for a first CL trophy ended in real drama. With Real 1-0 down to rivals Atletico Madrid, Ramos headed a last-second equaliser! Gareth Bale, Marcelo and Cristiano Ronaldo then scored in extra-time!

RAMOS SEASON BY SEASON

	2009-10	2010-11
La Liga games	33	31
La Liga goals	4	3
Trophies won	1	1

SAN SIRO SENSATION!

May 28, 2016

Two years after making Atletico fans cry in a Champo League final, Ramos did it all over again! He was Man of the Match and scored AGAIN as Real won the final in Milan's San Siro on penalties – Ramos also scored in the shootout!

WICKED IN WALES!

June 3, 2017

Ramos was ice-cool at Cardiff's Millennium Stadium as Real thrashed Juventus 4-1 in the 2017 final! He bossed Paulo Dybala and Gonzalo Higuain from start to finish, then picked up his third winners' medal!

SALAH'S WORST NIGHTMARE!

May 26, 2018

One of Ramos' most famous battles came against Liverpool in the 2018 Champions League final in Kiev. The Spanish rock's aggression and passion put Salah out of the game with an injury, then he helped Real grab a 3-1 victory!

2011-12	
La Liga games	34
La Liga goals	3
Trophies won	2

2012-13	
La Liga games	26
La Liga goals	4
Trophies won	1

2013-14	
La Liga games	32
La Liga goals	4
Trophies won	2

SERGIO'S SKILLS!

The Real Madrid and Spain legend is the ultimate centre-back – and a striker's worst nightmare! Get a load of his top skills...

POWER!

If you go into a 50-50 with Ramos, get ready to lose! His passion, determination and raw strength help him swat away strikers like they're flies! Sergio always puts his body on the line for his team!

SHOOTING!

He might be a legendary defender, but Ramos can also mix it up at the other end of the pitch. He could have been a striker with his clever movement and top finishing skills, plus he's an expert penalty-taker!

RAMOS
SEASON BY SEASON

	2014-15	2015-16
La Liga games	27	23
La Liga goals	4	2
Trophies won	2	1

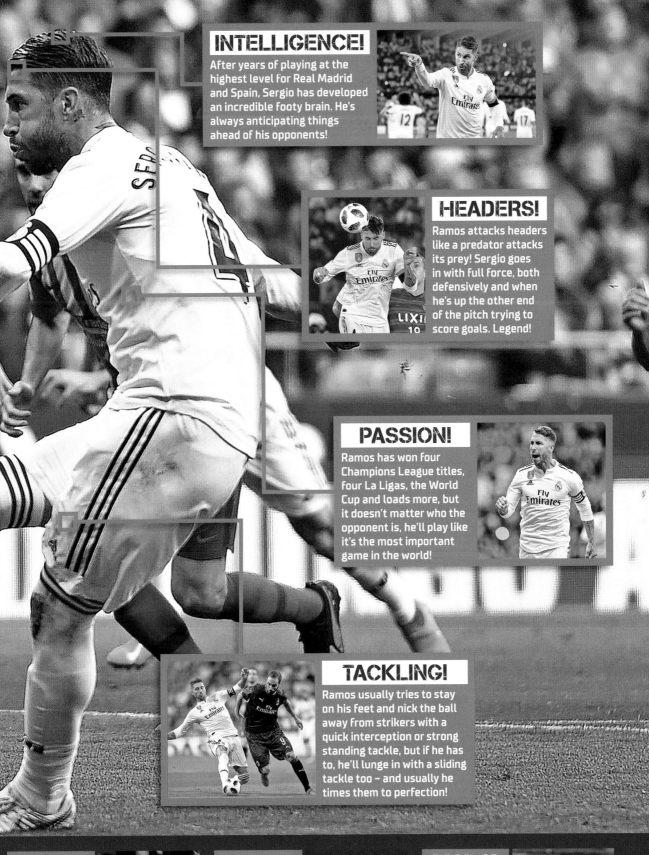

INTELLIGENCE!

After years of playing at the highest level for Real Madrid and Spain, Sergio has developed an incredible footy brain. He's always anticipating things ahead of his opponents!

HEADERS!

Ramos attacks headers like a predator attacks its prey! Sergio goes in with full force, both defensively and when he's up the other end of the pitch trying to score goals. Legend!

PASSION!

Ramos has won four Champions League titles, four La Ligas, the World Cup and loads more, but it doesn't matter who the opponent is, he'll play like it's the most important game in the world!

TACKLING!

Ramos usually tries to stay on his feet and nick the ball away from strikers with a quick interception or strong standing tackle, but if he has to, he'll lunge in with a sliding tackle too – and usually he times them to perfection!

2016-17

La Liga games	28
La Liga goals	7
Trophies won	4

2017-18

La Liga games	26
La Liga goals	4
Trophies won	4

2018-19

La Liga games	28
La Liga goals	6
Trophies won	1

WORDFIT

Fit 25 Champions-League winning Real stars into this grid!

MARCELO

Asensio	Casillas	Isco	Morata	Ramos
Bale	Coentrao	Khedira	Morientes	Raul
Benzema	Danilo	Kroos	Nacho	Ronaldo
Carvajal	Di Maria	Marcelo	Navas	Varane
Casemiro	Hierro	Modric	Pepe	Vazquez

SPOT THE DIFFERENCE

Study these Real Madrid v Atletico Madrid pictures carefully, then see if you can find the ten differences between them!

ANSWERS ON PAGE 60

JOVIC

GOAL MACHINE

Real Madrid supporters have a brand-new goal king to love!

There are loads of legendary strikers in world football who've been ripping nets for years, but we've needed some new goal kings to break through for a long time... step forward, Luka Jovic. The powerful finisher is part of a new breed of deadly net-busters – and he arrives at the Bernabeu with a red-hot reputation. After bossing the Bundesliga for Eintracht Frankfurt in 2018-19, and scoring ten goals in just 11 Europa League starts for the German side against the likes of Chelsea, Benfica, Inter, Lazio and Marseille, the Serbia striker is ready to step up to the next level. With a supply line of Eden Hazard, Luka Modric, Toni Kroos, Vinicius Jr. and Isco at Real Madrid, he could break goal records for fun in Spain – emulating some of the club's greatest goalscorers of all time along the way!

EUROPA LEAGUE KING

Jovic caught the eye of Real Madrid scouts last season with a series of outrageously good performances in the Europa League. He helped Bundesliga side Eintracht Frankfurt make a shock charge to the semi-finals with some massive goals, including an awesome dink against Italian giants Inter at the San Siro, before bagging in both legs against Chelsea in the semis. Total hero!

BENFICA REGRETS

Loads of clubs let youngsters leave on loan, but Benfica never realised they were losing a future superstar when they gave Jovic permission to join Frankfurt in 2017. The Germans signed him on loan for just £180,000 with an option to buy for £6.2 million. They made him a megastar, paid the agreed final transfer fee, then sold him shortly after to Real Madrid for £52 million. Monster profit!

THE NEW LEWANDOWSKI

Jovic has been compared to Bayern Munich star Robert Lewandowski. His mix of power, movement and surprise acceleration is very similar to the Poland hero, but it's his finishing that's drawn most comparisons. In the Europa League semi-final v Chelsea, there was a moment when Jovic went through on goal and his team-mates started celebrating before he scored. They knew it was going in!

DREAM MOVE

During his presentation at the Bernabeu, Jovic told the media he was the 'happiest kid in the world' and he'd 'give everything to help Real Madrid win more trophies.' When Eden Hazard joined for £89 million just days later, Jovic's transfer got completely overshadowed, but the Serbia goal machine will be out to do everything he can to prove he can be just as important a signing!

FACTPACK

Position: Striker
Country: Serbia
D.O.B: 23/12/1997
Height: 6ft
Boots: adidas X
Instagram: lukajovic

REAL MADRID

A

ALFREDO DI STEFANO!

Die-hard Madrid fans always argue about who their greatest ever player is, and Real icon Alfredo Di Stefano picks up loads of votes. The legendary striker was the star player as Real famously won the first five European Cups, scoring in all five finals. How incredible is that?

B

BERNABEU!

The Santiago Bernabeu is one of the most famous footy stadiums on the planet. Since opening in 1947, it has hosted a World Cup final, European Championship final, Champions League final, Copa Libertadores final, plus loads of epic games for Real Madrid!

C

CRISTIANO RONALDO!

Everyone knew Cristiano Ronaldo would be a big success at Real Madrid, but nobody thought his £80 million transfer from Man. United in 2009 would turn out to be the bargain of the century! CR7 became the club's all-time record scorer with 450 goals and helped them win four Champions League titles!

A-Z

Get a load of our ultimate guide to Real Madrid, then see if you can write your own A-Z of the club for the chance to win an awesome prize!

D

DAVID BECKHAM!

David Beckham was arguably the most famous person on the planet at the start of the millennium, and Real wanted a slice of the pie. Becks arrived at the Bernabeu from Man. United in 2003 and soon became La Liga's assist king with his legendary crossing skills!

E

EL CLASICO!

El Clasico is the most famous football game on the planet – fans from around the world stop whatever they're doing when Real Madrid battle Barcelona! Cristiano Ronaldo and Lionel Messi's epic rivalry dominated the headlines for years, but now a new wave of stars are ready to rip up the mega match!

F

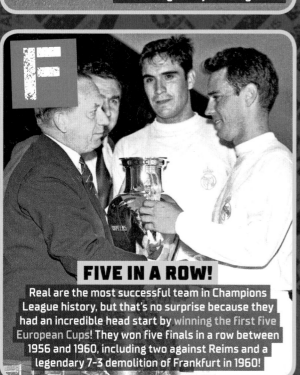

FIVE IN A ROW!

Real are the most successful team in Champions League history, but that's no surprise because they had an incredible head start by winning the first five European Cups! They won five finals in a row between 1956 and 1960, including two against Reims and a legendary 7-3 demolition of Frankfurt in 1960!

G

GALACTICOS!

Real Madrid have been nicknamed 'The Galacticos' in the media for their ruthless transfer activity over the years. When Ronaldo and Zinedine Zidane were the best players on the planet, Real fought hard to buy them. The same happened with Cristiano Ronaldo and Gareth Bale. They must have the best!

H

HAZARD!

The Bernabeu's latest Galactico is Belgium icon Eden Hazard. The devastating winger has been destroying Prem full-backs for years, but now he's ready to prove he's a Ballon d'Or contender at Real. He says Zinedine Zidane is his hero, which is the perfect way to impress his new boss!

I

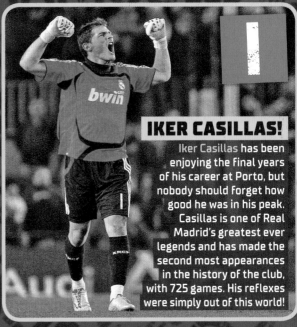

IKER CASILLAS!

Iker Casillas has been enjoying the final years of his career at Porto, but nobody should forget how good he was in his peak. Casillas is one of Real Madrid's greatest ever legends and has made the second most appearances in the history of the club, with 725 games. His reflexes were simply out of this world!

J

JUVENTUS!

Madrid have forged an interesting relationship with Juventus over the years. Predrag Mijatovic's goal gave Los Blancos a 1-0 win over Juve in the 1998 Champions League final, then a Cristiano Ronaldo masterclass helped Real crush them 4-1 in the 2017 final. Real also sold Ronaldo to Juventus in 2018!

K

KIEV!

Real picked up their 13th Champions League trophy in the 2018 final in Kiev. The Ukrainian city hosted an epic final, which saw super-sub Gareth Bale score one of the greatest goals we've ever seen! The Welshman's sick overhead kick helped Real beat Liverpool 3-1!

L

LUIS FIGO!

Luis Figo is one of the best wingers of the past 30 years, but he's more famous for the craziest transfer in footy history! The Portugal icon was Barcelona's star player, but stunned his team-mates and fans in 2000 by switching to rivals Real Madrid. Barça supporters now hate him!

M

MARCA!

Loads of newspapers and websites are famous for general footy news or transfer rumours, but Marca dedicate most of their content to Real Madrid. Marca love getting Los Blancos fans pumped by building up transfer rumours, and the club gives them awesome interview access to all of their star players!

O

OWEN!

Legendary England striker Michael Owen spent a season at Real Madrid in 2004-05. He turned up in Spain with a massive reputation after scoring loads for Liverpool and winning the Ballon d'Or but, after being restricted to sub appearances, he failed to make a big impact. He still scored 13 La Liga goals in just 20 starts though, including a strike v Barça in El Clasico!

N

NETHERLANDS!

Loads of Dutch dynamos have flown over from the Netherlands to rock the Bernabeu! Prem legends Arjen Robben and Ruud van Nistelrooy scored some huge goals for Los Blancos, while classy midfielder Clarence Seedorf won the Champions League with Real in 1998!

P

PUSKAS!

If you think Lionel Messi and Mohamed Salah have an awesome left foot, you should have seen Ferenc Puskas in action. His left foot was a mix of epic wizardry and hammer power! The Hungary legend scored FOUR goals in the 1960 European Cup final against Frankfurt, which is still a CL record!

Q — QUARTER-FINALS!

Real's last-16 defeat to Ajax in 2018-19 was the first time they'd lost at that stage of the Champions League since 2009-10. Los Blancos had played in eight CL quarter-finals in a row, including memorable wins v Atletico Madrid in 2014-15 and Bayern Munich in 2016-17!

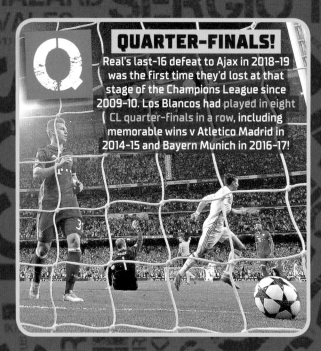

R

RAUL!

Raul is the Hollywood fairytale story in the incredible legacy of this great club. Born and raised in Madrid, the Spain star went on to become the all-time record appearance maker for his hometown team. His 741 games were full of class, creativity, leadership and elite finishing skills. What a total legend!

S — SERGIO RAMOS!

Love him or hate him, nobody can deny that Sergio Ramos is one of the greatest captains in footy history. Since Iker Casillas left the club, Ramos has captained Real to three CL titles in five seasons. Those three trophies include a memorable display in the 2018 final and a goal in the 2016 final!

T — THIRTEEN!

Real top the list of all-time Champions League winners by miles! Winning the first five tournaments gave them a massive head start, but since then they've won another eight! Bagging the tenth, 'La Decima', was a big deal for the club in 2014, before they went on to win three of the next four to move on to 13!

U — UK STARS!

Loads of players from the United Kingdom have ripped it up for Real Madrid over the years. Wales ace Gareth Bale is the most recent superstar, while David Beckham made a big impact in the mid-2000s. Ex-Liverpool heroes Michael Owen and Steve McManaman were also hits, while Laurie Cunningham became the first ever Englishman to play for Real in 1979!

V — VIEJO!

El Viejo Clasico is Spanish for 'The Old Classic', which is the name given to games between Real Madrid and Athletic Bilbao. It might sound crazy now, but this was THE game back in the early 1900s. They dominated Spanish footy and met in no less than eight Copa del Rey finals. Wow!

W — WALES!

Real Madrid have a close connection to the country of Wales! Dragons legend Gareth Bale scored the decisive goal to fire the club to 'La Decima' – their tenth Champions League trophy in 2014! They also won their 12th CL trophy in the country's capital Cardiff, while Welsh gaffer John Toshack was their manager twice!

X — X-FACTOR!

Real were falling behind the likes of Man. United, Bayern Munich and Juventus in the mid-1990s, so changed their transfer policy to get that X-factor back into the club. By the start of the 2000s, they were nicknamed The Galacticos after buying Zinedine Zidane, Luis Figo, Ronaldo and David Beckham!

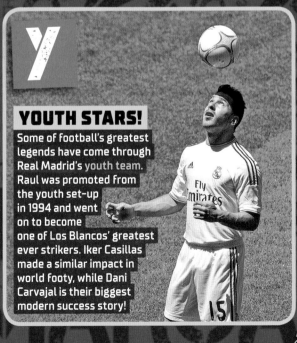

Y — YOUTH STARS!

Some of football's greatest legends have come through Real Madrid's youth team. Raul was promoted from the youth set-up in 1994 and went on to become one of Los Blancos' greatest ever strikers. Iker Casillas made a similar impact in world footy, while Dani Carvajal is their biggest modern success story!

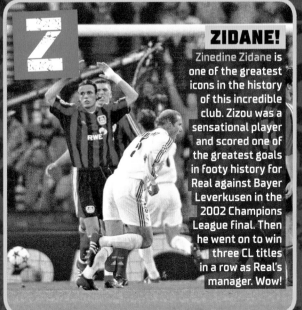

Z — ZIDANE!

Zinedine Zidane is one of the greatest icons in the history of this incredible club. Zizou was a sensational player and scored one of the greatest goals in footy history for Real against Bayer Leverkusen in the 2002 Champions League final. Then he went on to win three CL titles in a row as Real's manager. Wow!

WRITE YOUR OWN
REAL MADRID A-Z

Fill in your own Real A-Z and you could win a year's free subscription to MATCH magazine!

A.

B.

C.

D.

E.

F.

G.

H.

I.

J.

K.

L.

M.

N.

O.

P.

Q.

R.

S.

T.

U.

V.

W.

X.

Y.

Z.

NAME:

DATE OF BIRTH:

ADDRESS:

MOBILE:

EMAIL:

It doesn't matter if you pick some of the same words as MATCH, but try to research and think of at least five new ones!

Photocopy this page, write down your own Real Madrid A-Z, fill out your contact details and send your entry to: **MATCH Real Madrid 2020 Annual, Kelsey Media, Regent House, Welbeck Way, Peterborough, Cambs, PE2 7WH** *Winner will be picked at random. Closing date: Jan. 31, 2020.*

REAL'S BEST GOAL EVER?

We've picked out four of the greatest goals in *REAL MADRID*'s history! Which one do you think is the best?

BRILLIANT BALE!

Welsh legend Gareth Bale has scored some mind-blowing long shots and dribbling goals for Real Madrid, but his most famous strike came in the 2018 Champions League final against Liverpool. He swivelled on the edge of the box to slam home an overhead-kick volley into the top corner. Wow!

ZIZOU'S ELITE VOLLEY!

Zinedine Zidane was the coolest midfielder on the planet before he became the coolest manager on the planet! His finest moment came in the 2002 Champions League final when he met Roberto Carlos' looping cross and pinged an ace volley into the top corner with his weaker left foot!

RED-HOT REDONDO!

This goal was so great simply because the assist was so good! Argentina's playmaking CM Fernando Redondo embarrassed Man. United defender Henning Berg on the left wing with a backheel nutmeg, then set up Raul for an easy tap-in as Real beat The Red Devils 3-2 at Old Trafford in 2000!

RONALDO SILENCES JUVE!

Gareth Bale wasn't the only Real Madrid star to score a spectacular overhead kick in 2017-18! Cristiano Ronaldo did exactly the same against Juventus in the quarter-finals, which stunned the Turin fans so much they all stood up and clapped. It worked... he joined them three months later!

41

ULTIMATE

HEADERS
CRISTIANO RONALDO

Cristiano Ronaldo is one of the greatest finishers in footy history, but one of his most underrated skills is his heading ability. CR7 leaps in the air like an NBA star, then busts nets with heading accuracy and power. His header v Barcelona in the 2011 Copa del Rey final was unbelievable!

YOU PICK:

REFLEXES
IKER CASILLAS

During his time at Real Madrid when he was at his absolute peak, Iker Casillas was a mix of Jan Oblak, David de Gea and Spider-Man! The iconic Real Madrid and Spain legend was a forward's worst nightmare – he dominated his 18-yard box with bravery and lightning-fast reflexes!

YOU PICK:

DRIBBLING
RONALDO

The original Ronaldo from Brazil was one of the greatest footy stars the world has ever seen! R9 arrived at the Bernabeu shortly after winning the 2002 World Cup and Golden Boot with Brazil, then quickly showed his new fans a range of dribbling and stepovers from another planet!

YOU PICK:

PASSING
ZINEDINE ZIDANE

The current Real Madrid gaffer gets a spot in our Ultimate Player – and he could have had a few more! His vision and heading were also world class, but it was his passing that made him a true footy icon. He inspired many of the midfielders you see today with clever, positive passing!

YOU PICK:

PLAYER!

to create an all-time superstar – and you can do the same!

VISION
ALFREDO DI STEFANO

Legendary Real Madrid icon Alfredo Di Stefano was famous for being the complete footballer. He absolutely destroyed teams in the 1950s and 1960s with his incredible finishing and skill, but it was his footy brain and eagle-eyed vision that made him a true, one-of-a-kind superstar!

YOU PICK:

TACKLING
SERGIO RAMOS

Rival supporters might not like Sergio Ramos, but that's only because they're jealous he doesn't play for them! Every team needs a player like Ramos in their side. He'll do anything to win, is a magnificent leader and reads the game brilliantly. On top form, even the best goal machines can't get past him!

YOU PICK:

SPEED
GARETH BALE

Gareth Bale joined Real Madrid in 2013 with an incredible reputation from his time at Tottenham. He changed the game with his electric pace and direct dribbling style, then proved it in his first season at Real with an outrageous sprint and finish in the Copa del Rey final v Barcelona!

YOU PICK:

FINISHING
FERENC PUSKAS

Some of the greatest strikers in football history have played for Real Madrid, so this spot could've gone to anyone. Ronaldo, Raul, Cristiano Ronaldo and Alfredo Di Stefano were all absolutely lethal goalscorers, but Hungarian hero Ferenc Puskas' left foot was one of the deadliest of all time!

YOU PICK:

STAT ATTACK!

ALL-TIME APPEARANCES

	PLAYER	GAMES
1	Raul	741
2	Iker Casillas	725
3	Manuel Sanchis	710
4	Santillana	645
5	Sergio Ramos	606

ALL-TIME TOP SCORERS

	PLAYER	GOALS
1	Cristiano Ronaldo	450
2	Raul	323
3	Alfredo Di Stefano	308
4	Santillana	290
5	Ferenc Puskas	242

Get a load of REAL MADRID's *biggest signings, longest winning streaks, record scorers, social media fans and more!*

15

Zinedine Zidane has a long way to go to become Real's longest-serving manager. Miguel Munoz spent 15 years at the club as gaffer over two spells!

Real Madrid's record victory in a competitive game actually came in El Clasico! They smashed Barcelona 11-1 in the 1942-43 Copa del Rey!

ANO 1943

11-1, EL REAL INFLIGE AL BARCELONA UNA DERROTA SIN PRECEDENTES
¡Y ESO QUE AL CONJUNTO BLANCO LE ANULARON CUATRO GOLES!

11

LA LIGA POSITION
LAST 20 SEASONS

1999-2000	2000-2001	2001-2002	2002-2003	2003-2004	2004-2005	2005-2006	2006-2007	2007-2008	2008-2009	2009-2010	2010-2011	2011-2012	2012-2013	2013-2014	2014-2015	2015-2016	2016-2017	2017-2018	2018-2019
5th	1st	3rd	1st	4th	2nd	2nd	1st	1st	2nd	2nd	2nd	3rd	2nd	2nd	2nd	1st	1st	3rd	3rd

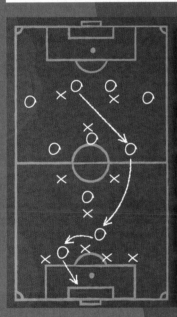

61

Cristiano Ronaldo scored a jaw-dropping 61 goals for Real Madrid in all comps in 2014-15, including 48 in La Liga. Unbelievable!

10

Countries represented in 2018-19 squad

Costa Rica

Spain

France

Dominican Rep.

Germany

Croatia

Wales

Belgium

Brazil

Uruguay

LA LIGA STREAKS!

LONGEST WINNING STREAK
16 matches

LONGEST UNBEATEN STREAK
28 matches

LONGEST SCORING STREAK
54 matches

LONGEST LOSING STREAK
5 matches

12

Chile legend Ivan Zamorano scored after just 12 seconds against Sevilla in 1994. It's the fastest goal in Real Madrid's history!

BIGGEST TRANSFERS

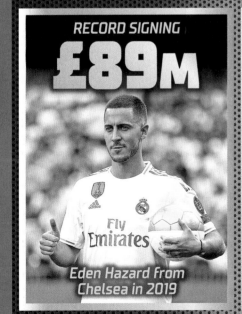

RECORD SIGNING

£89M

Eden Hazard from Chelsea in 2019

RECORD SALE

£99.2M

Cristiano Ronaldo to Juventus in 2018

facebook
110+
MILLION **Likes**

73+
MILLION FOLLOWERS

twitter
52+
MILLION FOLLOWERS

Stats only include official matches. Correct up to start of the 2019-20 season.

MILITAO

REAL'S NEW ROCK

The dynamite defender is set to rule the Bernabeu for years!

Since 2015-16, the performance of Real Madrid's defence has steadily declined. They've continued to ship more goals as each year goes by, culminating in 46 conceded in 2018-19 – their worst record for a decade. While there's no doubting the individual ability of defenders Sergio Ramos, Raphael Varane and Dani Carvajal, who've rocked the famous white shirts for years, there's obvious cause for concern – and that's where Eder Militao comes in. He was one of the most sought after defenders in world football before Real won the race for his signature, so he's got bags of ability and loads of potential. While Real's past philosophy was to sign Galacticos who rule the attacking third of the pitch, we're now witnessing the beginning of an era where they're rebuilding with Galacticos in defence... starting with Militao!

RAPID RISE

Eder Militao started his career with Brazilian giants Sao Paulo and quickly made a name for himself as a future superstar. Most centre-backs need five or six years' experience at the top level to become an elite defender, but Militao quickly proved he had the footy brain and raw talent to be a proper star, securing a massive move to Portuguese giants Porto at the tender age of 20!

SAMBA WONDERKID

Militao won his first Brazil cap just one month after finalising his big move to Porto, then went on to bag a Copa America winners' medal last summer, coming off the bench in the 3-1 final victory over Peru. Add that success to his wicked debut season with Porto and sealing a massive £45 million move to Real Madrid, it's safe to say 2019 was a good year for the Samba Star!

RAMOS REPLACEMENT?

Sergio Ramos turns 34 in 2020 and, although he's still got a couple of decent seasons left in him, Real need to have one eye on his replacement. However, they won't need to scout a new player for that, because Militao already looks like the ideal successor. Like Ramos, he can play at right-back as well as centre-back, and that sort of versatility will make him a very useful player!

THE NEW VAN DIJK?

Although Militao's earmarked as Ramos' replacement, his style of play is much more like Liverpool's CL winner Virgil van Dijk. Like VVD, Militao is a proper defender, athletic and comfortable with the ball at his feet. Real Madrid fans will love his aggressive heading style, power and no-nonsense tackling, but will be even more in awe when they see him launching attacks from the back!

FACTPACK

Position: Centre-back

Country: Brazil

D.O.B: 18/01/1998

Height: 6ft 1in

Boots: adidas Nemeziz

Instagram: edermilitaooficial13

CROSSWORD

Use the clues below to fill in this rock-hard Real Madrid puzzle!

ACROSS

1. Legendary Real Madrid and Hungary striker, Ferenc _ _ _ _ _ _! (6)

5. BT Sport pundit who scored for Real Madrid in the 2000 Champions League Final, _ _ _ _ _ McManaman! (5)

6. Vinicius Jr. and Rodrygo were born in this country! (6)

9. Real Madrid's second top goalscorer of all time! (4)

11. El Viejo Clasico is the name of Real Madrid's clashes against this club! (8,6)

13. Team that knocked Real Madrid out of the 2018-19 Champions League! (4)

16. Spanish side that Real signed Sergio Ramos from way back in 2005! (7)

17. Real Madrid gaffer before Zinedine Zidane returned in 2019, Santiago _ _ _ _ _ _! (6)

18. Real Madrid won the 2002 Champions League Final in this British city! (7)

DOWN

2. City that Real won the 2018 Champions League Final in! (4)

3. Country that new signing Ferland Mendy plays for! (6)

4. Real's finishing position in La Liga in 2018-19! (5)

5. New signing Luka Jovic plays international footy for this country! (6)

6. Los Blancos play their home games at this mind-blowing stadium! (8)

7. Thibaut Courtois and Eden Hazard play international footy for this country! (7)

8. Real have beaten two La Liga teams in a Champions League final – Atletico Madrid and _ _ _ _ _ _ _ _! (8)

10. German midfield maestro who wears the No.8 shirt for Real Madrid! (4,5)

12. Real controversially bought this Portugal winger from arch-rivals Barcelona way back in 2000! (4,4)

14. Real sold Cristiano Ronaldo to this massive Italian club in 2018! (8)

15. Legendary Real Madrid and Brazil left-back, Roberto _ _ _ _ _ _! (6)

NAME THE TEAM

Can you remember the stars that lined up in Real Madrid's 3-1 win against Liverpool in the 2018 Champions League final?

1. Goalkeeper

2. Centre-back

3. Midfielder

4. Centre-back

5. Striker

6. Forward

7. Def. midfielder

8. Left-back

9. Right-back

10. Midfielder

11. Midfielder

ANSWERS ON PAGE 60

CLUB HISTORY

REAL MADRID THROUGH THE YEARS!

A ROYAL STAMP!

In 1920, King Alfonso XIII of Spain gave the club permission to change their name to Real Madrid. 'Real' means 'Royal' in Spanish and the king was a big footy fan. They had to change their name again during the Spanish Civil War, but after that they were Real Madrid forever!

A NEW TEAM IS BORN!

Real Madrid were founded in 1902 by president Juan Padros, but they weren't called Real Madrid at the start. Los Blancos' first club name was Madrid FC and they started with immediate success, winning four of the first six Copa del Rey tournaments!

1920

1956

THE GOLDEN ERA BEGINS!

UEFA put together the first-ever Champions League tournament in 1955-56 with some of Europe's best clubs. It was called the European Cup back then, and Real were the first club to win the famous trophy. Los Blancos beat Reims 4-3 in the final!

1947

1902

HOME SWEET HOME!

New Real Madrid chief Santiago Bernabeu Yeste rebuilt the club after the Spanish Civil War and named the world-famous stadium after himself! It opened in 1947 and quickly became one of the greatest sporting arenas on the planet!

1960

SEVENTH HEAVEN!

Real built on their 1956 success by winning the next three European Cups! They arrived at Hampden Park in Glasgow in 1960 aiming to win five in a row – and did exactly that with one of the most famous club displays of all time. They smashed Eintracht Frankfurt 7-3 in the final!

BACK ON TOP!

Benfica, AC Milan and Inter temporarily ended Real Madrid's European domination, but Los Blancos were back on top in 1966. Amancio and Fernando Serena scored as Real beat Partizan 2-1 at Heysel Stadium in Brussels!

WICKED WONDERKIDS!

After a few quiet years, Real Madrid started dominating La Liga again with a bunch of class homegrown heroes straight from their academy. Emilio Butragueno, Michel, Manuel Sanchis and Martin Vazquez helped the club win five league titles in a row between 1985-86 and 1989-90!

SHOCK SIGNING!

Two months after winning their eighth Champions League title, Real shocked the world by signing the star player of deadly rivals Barcelona! Luis Figo was one of the biggest heroes at Euro 2000, and Real stunned everyone by signing him for a world-record £37 million!

2000

2001

1986

1998

1966

THE GALACTICOS!

Real were desperate to be the biggest club on the planet again, and they did that by signing the world's most famous stars! France maestro Zinedine Zidane arrived in 2001 for another world-record fee, and Brazil hitman Ronaldo signed 12 months later to make Real the coolest team around!

1980

LA LIGA DOMINATION!

After 1966, Real had a barren run in the European Cup, but they continued their dominance of La Liga in the 1970s. They won five out of six Spanish titles between 1974-75 and 1979-80, with Jose Antonio Camacho and Pirri the superstars of the team!

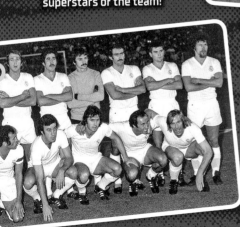

32 YEARS OF HURT!

Real had dominated the early years of the Champions League, but they hadn't won the famous trophy for 32 years heading into the 1998 final! Predrag Mijatovic's goal ended that run as Madrid beat Juventus 1-0!

Real hadn't won a major trophy for four years before ending that run with a dramatic La Liga triumph in 2006-07! They needed to beat Real Mallorca on the final day to lift the trophy, but went 1-0 down! Jose Antonio Reyes, who was on loan from Arsenal, saved the day with an epic double – and Real were champs!

100 CLUB!

Los Blancos dominated La Liga in 2011-12 – they won the title with 100 points, nine points clear of rivals Barcelona! It was also an incredible season for star man Cristiano Ronaldo, who scored 46 league goals!

2012

ZIDANE RULES HAMPDEN!

Zinedine Zidane scored a volley from another planet as Real Madrid bagged their ninth Champo League title at Hampden Park in Scotland. If you haven't seen Zizou's wondergoal against Bayer Leverkusen before, stop what you're doing right now and find it on YouTube!

2007

2009

2014

2003

2002

CRISTIANO ARRIVES!

Real Madrid signed Cristiano Ronaldo from Man. United in 2009 and changed the face of their team for the next decade! The Bernabeu was filled with celebrating fans for his presentation, and those supporters would go on to see CR7 bag 450 goals for Los Blancos!

BECKHAM SIGNS!

Just when you thought Real couldn't fit any more superstars into their star-studded squad, Los Blancos shocked the world by signing David Beckham from Man. United! Becks was probably the most famous athlete on the planet in 2003 and made Real even bigger!

LA DECIMA!

Real fans had been dreaming of 'La Decima' for 12 years, and it finally arrived with a dramatic win against Atletico Madrid in Lisbon. 'La Decima' was the term used for Los Blancos' tenth Champo League title – and it was now official!

THE ITALIAN JOB!

Two years after breaking the hearts of massive rivals Atletico Madrid in the Champions League Final, Real Madrid did the exact same thing at the San Siro in Milan. Sergio Ramos scored as the final finished 1-1, before five perfect penalties won the shootout and gave Real title number 11!

LUCKY NUMBER 13!

Los Blancos' European domination continued in 2018 with a mind-blowing 13th Champo League title! Gareth Bale scored one of the greatest goals in footy history with an unbelievable overhead kick, as Real beat Liverpool 3-1 in Kiev!

2019

2018

2016

2017

WIZARDS IN WALES!

Real Madrid lit up Cardiff's Millennium Stadium on June 3, 2017 with a sensational 4-1 victory against Juventus. It was their 12th CL title and confirmation that they were the best team in Europe. Cristiano Ronaldo was the star of the show with a lethal double!

RETURN OF THE KING!

Real Madrid fans were left heartbroken when icon Zinedine Zidane quit as manager in 2018, but after unsuccessful spells in the hotseat from Julen Lopetegui and Santiago Solari, Bernabeu chiefs convinced the Frenchman to make a triumphant return!

TOP 5...
EL CLASICO HEROES!

Check out five superstars from REAL MADRID's history who've helped Los Blancos totally destroy rivals Barcelona in the past!

5 ZINEDINE ZIDANE

FAB FACT!
In the three games that Zizou scored against Barcelona, Real never lost!

When Real Madrid and Barcelona met in the 2001-02 Champions League semi-final, the media called it the 'Match of the Century'. The whole world was watching and legendary France star Zinedine Zidane sealed victory in the first leg with an incredible display at the Nou Camp. He scored a cracker in a 2-0 win!

EL CLASICO STATS

GAMES		WINS		GOALS	
	11		4		3

4 ALFREDO DI STEFANO

FAB FACT!
Barcelona and Real were locked in a transfer war for Di Stefano in the 1950s!

Alfredo Di Stefano is one of the greatest players in footy history – and El Clasico was his playground! The Real legend loved scoring against his team's biggest rivals, and netted a famous double against Barça in the 1959-60 European Cup semi-final. Surprisingly though, he never scored a hat-trick against them!

EL CLASICO STATS

GAMES		WINS		GOALS	
	29		16		18

EL CLASICO VILLAINS!

Check out these five El Clasico villains, too. Boo!

LIONEL MESSI

Credit where it's due... Leo is the top scorer in El Clasico history with 26 goals – he's terrorised the Real Madrid defence numerous times!

RONALDINHO

Brazil magician Ronaldinho was once clapped by the Real Madrid supporters after a mind-blowing double at the Bernabeu!

3 GARETH BALE

FAB FACT!
Bale's one Clasico assist came in the only La Liga game he's won v Barça!

The Welsh wing wizard joined Real from Tottenham for a world-record £85.3 million in 2013, and quickly realised how popular he'd be if he scored in El Clasico. In his first season at the club, he bagged the winning goal against Barcelona in the Copa del Rey Final – he sprinted from one end of the pitch to the other, finished brilliantly and became an instant legend!

EL CLASICO STATS

GAMES		WINS		GOALS	
	14		3		2

2 RAUL

FAB FACT!
Raul scored a double four times in El Clasico – he loved the big games!

Raul came through Real Madrid's youth academy, so El Clasico meant more to him than most players. His grace and class was mixed with pure passion and aggression when he faced Barcelona. His most famous Clasico moment arrived during the 1999-2000 season, when he scored at the Nou Camp and told the 100,000 home fans to be quiet with a 'Ssshhh' celebration!

EL CLASICO STATS

GAMES		WINS		GOALS	
	37		11		15

1 CRISTIANO RONALDO

FAB FACT!
CR7 headed an extra-time winner v Barcelona in the 2011 Copa del Rey Final!

The iconic Portugal megastar has had some epic El Clasico moments over the years! There are too many to mention, but our favourite goal was an equaliser at the Nou Camp in 2012-13. Lionel Messi had just put Barcelona 2-1 up, but CR7 silenced the home crowd with his second goal of the match. This was also the night that Ronaldo started his famous 'calm down' celebration!

EL CLASICO STATS

GAMES		WINS		GOALS	
	33		9		18

ANDRES INIESTA

The Spain legend was Real Madrid's nemesis in midfield battles during the late 2000s and early 2010s. What a player!

GERARD PIQUE

Pique's mega proud of his Catalan roots, and loves winding up Real Madrid fans with controversial comments in the media!

CARLES PUYOL

The passionate centre-back was 'Mr. Barcelona' during his playing days, and was a real hate figure for Madrid fans!

2019-20 FIRST TEAM SQUAD

GOALKEEPERS

No.	Player	La Liga Games/Goals 2018-19	Signed from
1	Alphonse Areola	N/A	PSG, 2019
13	Thibaut Courtois	27/0	Chelsea, 2018

Courtois

DEFENDERS

No.	Player	La Liga Games/Goals 2018-19	Signed from
2	Dani Carvajal	24/1	B. Leverkusen, 2013
3	Eder Militao	N/A	Porto, 2019
4	Sergio Ramos	28/6	Sevilla, 2005
5	Raphael Varane	32/2	Lens, 2011
6	Nacho	20/0	Academy
12	Marcelo	23/2	Fluminense, 2007
19	Alvaro Odriozola	14/0	Real Sociedad, 2016
23	Ferland Mendy	N/A	Lyon, 2019

Odriozola

MIDFIELDERS

No.	Player	La Liga Games/Goals 2018-19	Signed from
8	Toni Kroos	28/0	Bayern Munich, 2014
10	Luka Modric	34/3	Tottenham, 2012
14	Casemiro	29/3	Sao Paulo, 2013
15	Federico Valverde	16/0	Penarol, 2016
16	James Rodriguez	N/A	Monaco, 2014
20	Marco Asensio	30/1	Real Mallorca, 2014
21	Brahim Diaz	9/1	Man. City, 2019
22	Isco	27/3	Malaga, 2013

Vinicius Jr.

FORWARDS

No.	Player	La Liga Games/Goals 2018-19	Signed from
7	Eden Hazard	N/A	Chelsea, 2019
9	Karim Benzema	36/21	Lyon, 2009
11	Gareth Bale	29/8	Tottenham, 2013
17	Lucas Vazquez	31/1	Academy
18	Luka Jovic	N/A	E. Frankfurt, 2019
24	Mariano Diaz	13/3	Lyon, 2018
25	Vinicius Jr.	18/2	Flamengo, 2018
27	Rodrygo	N/A	Santos, 2019

MEET THE MANAGER

ZINEDINE ZIDANE

We take a closer look at the iconic **REAL MADRID** manager...

LEGENDARY PLAYER!

Zidane was the greatest footballer in the world when he arrived at Real Madrid back in 2001, and Los Blancos helped him get even better. Fresh from winning a World Cup 1998 and Euro 2000 double with France, Zizou totally rocked the Bernabeu with grace, class, style and swagger!

LEGEND TURNED BOSS!

Loads of media critics, footy fans and social media trolls were critical of Real Madrid for hiring Zidane as their gaffer in 2016 because he didn't have much managerial experience. Fast-forward five months and he was masterminding Real's 11th Champions League final win over rivals Atletico Madrid in Milan!

THREE IN A ROW!

After winning his first Champions League trophy as manager in 2016, Zizou turned into one of the biggest names in football management. He helped Real smash Juventus 4-1 in the 2017 CL final, then bagged an historic third title in a row with a 3-1 win against Liverpool in 2018!

"Every piece of advice he gives you is like gold dust and it helps you improve on the pitch."
Luka Modric
Real Madrid midfielder

COMEBACK KING!

Zizou stunned Los Blancos chiefs and fans in 2018 by leaving the club shortly after guiding them to a famous 13th CL title. Real sold hero Cristiano Ronaldo and had a shocking 2018-19 season, so had no choice but to convince the king to become gaffer at the Bernabeu again!

STAT ATTACK!

Take a look at some of Zidane's best stats as Real Madrid gaffer...

0
Zizou's never failed to win the Champions League as manager – Real have won it every year he's been in charge!

106
Real scored 106 La Liga goals during Zidane's first full season in charge, as they stormed to the 2016-17 title!

27
Julen Lopetegui and Santiago Solari were in charge of just 27 La Liga games between them before Real re-hired Zizou!

13
Zidane's helped Real Madrid win three Champions League titles as boss, including an historic 13th in 2018!

REAL'S NEXT GENERATION!

We take a closer look at five of the hottest young footy talents ready to break through at the Bernabeu over the next couple of years!

BRAHIM DIAZ
MIDFIELDER

Diaz's contract was running down at Man. City, so Real pounced to snap him up for a bargain price. The Premier League champions could regret that, because Brahim has the dribbling skills and vision to become a midfield genius!

TOP SKILL: Creativity

POTENTIAL
8/10

POTENTIAL
7/10

LUCA ZIDANE
Goalkeeper

Zinedine Zidane handed son Luca his debut during his first spell in charge of Real, then started him again last season when he returned to the club! The keeper has a big future, and could be ready for the first team once he returns from a season-long loan at Racing Santander!

TOP SKILL: Reflexes

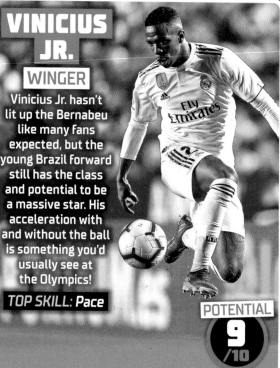

VINICIUS JR.
WINGER

Vinicius Jr. hasn't lit up the Bernabeu like many fans expected, but the young Brazil forward still has the class and potential to be a massive star. His acceleration with and without the ball is something you'd usually see at the Olympics!

TOP SKILL: Pace

POTENTIAL
9/10

POTENTIAL 10/10

RODRYGO
WINGER

Real signed Rodrygo for £40 million last summer and he could be worth double that in a few years' time! The wicked wonderkid has all the flair and tricks you'd expect from a Braziian winger, and could become a global superstar!

TOP SKILL: Tricks

TAKEFUSA KUBO
FORWARD

Kubo is on loan at Real Mallorca for the 2019-20 season, but we're expecting the Japan wonderkid to make a breakthrough into Real Madrid's first team very soon! He played his first game in the J-League aged just 15 and has already made his senior debut for his country, so his potential is absolutely massive!

TOP SKILL: Confidence

POTENTIAL 9/10

LEGENDS OF THE YOUTH TEAM!

These five superstars proved it's possible to go from the Real Madrid youth team to total Los Blancos legends!

Manuel Sanchis
Legendary defender who was a major part of Real's young team full of local talent in the 1980s!

Guti
Creative genius and classy midfielder. Go on YouTube to watch his mind-blowing backheel assist for Real!

Raul
Unbelievable success story who would be Real's top scorer ever if it wasn't for a guy called Cristiano Ronaldo!

Iker Casillas
Became a first-team icon, captain of the club and an expert at stopping shots with his unreal reflexes!

Emilio Butragueno
Deadly striker Butragueno was nicknamed 'The Vulture' for his lethal goalscoring style in the 1980s!

Brain-Buster P16

1. 13
2. Iker Casillas
3. Gareth Bale
4. Costa Rica
5. No.10
6. Marco Asensio
7. Barcelona
8. Tottenham
9. Casemiro
10. Cardiff

Wordfit P30

Name The Team P49

1. Keylor Navas
2. Sergio Ramos
3. Toni Kroos
4. Raphael Varane
5. Karim Benzema
6. Cristiano Ronaldo
7. Casemiro
8. Marcelo
9. Dani Carvajal
10. Isco
11. Luka Modric

Spot The Difference P31

Crossword P48

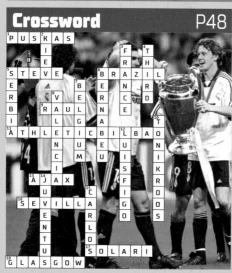

Face In The Crowd P17

ROLL OF HONOUR

FIFA CLUB OF THE CENTURY
2000

CHAMPIONS LEAGUE
1955–56, 1956–57, 1957–58, 1958–59,
1959–60, 1965–66, 1997–98, 1999–2000,
2001–02, 2013–14, 2015–16, 2016–17, 2017–18

FIFA CLUB WORLD CUP
2014, 2016, 2017, 2018

INTERCONTINENTAL CUP
1960, 1998, 2002

UEFA CUP
1984–85, 1985–86

EUROPEAN SUPER CUP
2002, 2014, 2016, 2017

LA LIGA
1931–32, 1932–33, 1953–54, 1954–55, 1956–57,
1957–58, 1960–61, 1961–62, 1962–63, 1963–64,
1964–65, 1966–67, 1967–68, 1968–69, 1971–72,
1974–75, 1975–76, 1977–78, 1978–79, 1979–80,
1985–86, 1986–87, 1987–88, 1988–89, 1989–90,
1994–95, 1996–97, 2000–01, 2002–03, 2006–07,
2007–08, 2011–12, 2016–17

COPA DEL REY
1904–05, 1905–06, 1906–07, 1907–08, 1916–17,
1933–34, 1935–36, 1945–46, 1946–47, 1961–62,
1969–70, 1973–74, 1974–75, 1979–80, 1981–82,
1988–89, 1992–93, 2010–11, 2013–14

SPANISH SUPER CUP
1988, 1989, 1990, 1993, 1997, 2001, 2003, 2008,
2012, 2017

SPANISH LEAGUE CUP
1984–85

SMALL WORLD CUP
1952, 1956

LATIN CUP
1955, 1957

REGIONAL CHAMPIONSHIP
1903–04, 1904–05, 1905–06, 1906–07, 1907–08,
1912–13, 1915–16, 1916–17, 1917–18, 1919–20, 1921–22,
1922–23, 1923–24, 1925–26, 1926–27, 1928–29,
1929–30, 1930–31

MANCOMUNADOS TROPHY
1931–32, 1932–33, 1933–34, 1934–35, 1935–36

COPA IBEROAMERICANA
1994

COPA EVA DUARTE
1947